Science Vocabulary Readers

The Planets

Jeff Bauer

SCHOLASTIC INC.

NEW YORK • TORONTO • LONDON • AUCKLAND • SYDNEY
MEXICO CITY • NEW DELHI • HONG KONG • BUENOS AIRES

ISBN-13: 978-0-545-00733-7 / ISBN-10: 0-545-00733-X

Photos Credits:
Cover: © NASA/Science Source/Photo Researchers; title page: © Sightseeing Archive/Getty Images; contents page, from top: © Tony Freeman/Photo Edit Inc., © William Radcliff/Getty Images, © NASA/ Science Source/Photo Researchers; page 4: © Roger Ressmeyer/Corbis; page 5: © Tony Freeman/Photo Edit Inc.; page 5, inset: © Digital Vision/Getty Images; pages 6–7: © William Radcliff/Getty Images; page 8: © William Radcliff/Getty Images; page 9: © NASA/Roger Ressmeyer/Corbis; page 9, inset: © NASA/ Roger Ressmeyer/Corbis; page 10: © Geosphere Project/Photo Researchers; page 11 © NASA; page 11, inset: © Purestock/Getty Images; page 12: © StockTrek/Getty Images; page 12, inset: © Photolink/Getty Images; page 13: © NASA/Science Source/Photo Researchers; page 14, from top: © Space Telescope Science Institute/NASA/Photo Researchers, © NASA; page 15: © Shigemi Numazawal/Atlas Photo Bank/ Photo Researchers; back cover: © StockTrek Images/RF/Getty Images.

Photo research by Dwayne Howard
Design by Holly Grundon

Copyright © 2007 by Lefty's Editorial Services
All rights reserved. Published by Scholastic Inc.

SCHOLASTIC and associated logos are trademarks and/or registered trademarks of Scholastic Inc.

12 11 10   11 12/0

Printed in the U.S.A.   40
First printing, December 2007

Contents

Chapter 1

What Is a Planet?

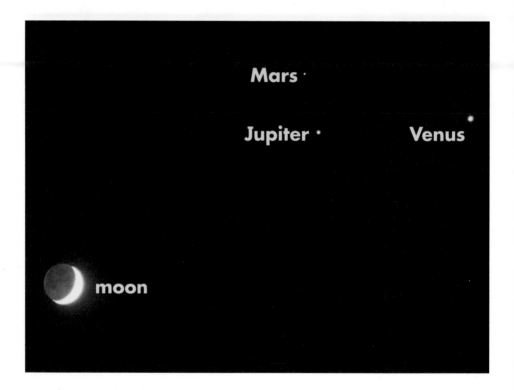

Take a look at this picture. You can see the moon, right? But there is something else glowing in the night sky. Those tiny dots of light are planets!

Venus looks like this through a telescope. It travels nearly 80,000 miles per hour.

You can get a great look at some of the planets with a **telescope**. Planets are round like balls. They travel through space at amazing speeds.

sun Mercury Earth Jupiter

Venus Mars

My Very Eager Mother Just Served Us Noodles. This sentence can help you remember the eight planets in order. My = Mercury, Very = Venus, and so on.

Guess what? Our home, the Earth, is a planet! The Earth is one of eight planets. Some are bigger than the Earth and some are smaller. All of the planets **orbit** around the sun.

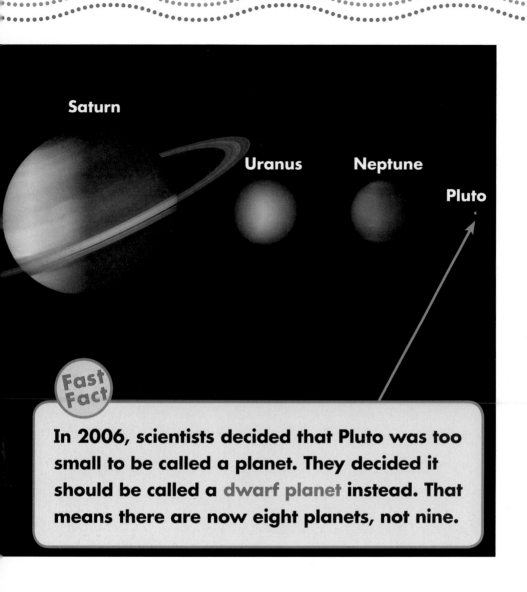

Saturn

Uranus

Neptune

Pluto

Fast Fact

In 2006, scientists decided that Pluto was too small to be called a planet. They decided it should be called a dwarf planet instead. That means there are now eight planets, not nine.

The four planets closest to the sun are called the inner planets. The other four are called the outer planets. Let's take a space tour to learn all about them.

Chapter 2

The Inner Planets

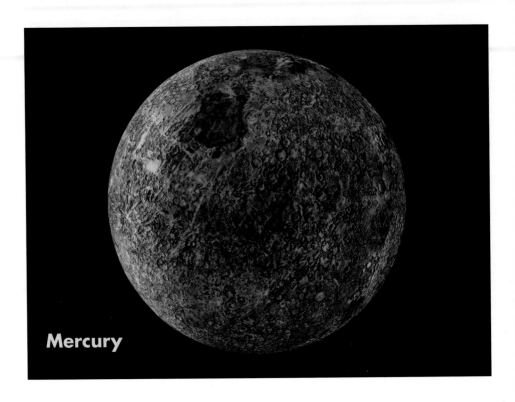

Mercury

The planet Mercury is closest to the sun. It gets super-hot during the day. The surface of Mercury is covered with craters just like the moon.

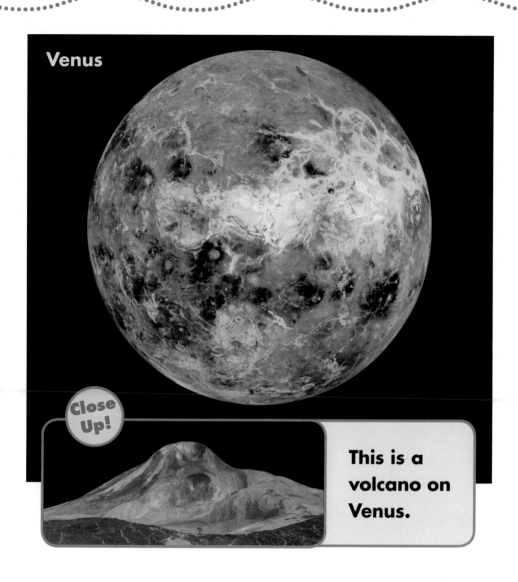

Venus

Close Up!

This is a volcano on Venus.

The planet Venus has lots of volcanoes. The air is filled with thick clouds of poisonous gas. The gas smells like rotten eggs. Yuck!

This is Africa.

Earth

The planet Earth is just the right distance from the sun for living things. It is not too hot or too cold. More than six-and-a-half billion people live here!

Mars

Fast Fact

This space probe is called the Mars Rover.

The planet Mars has a reddish color. **Space probes** have visited there, but nobody was onboard. The probes took pictures and sent them back to Earth.

Chapter 3

The Outer Planets

Close Up!

This is one of Jupiter's moons.

Jupiter

The planet Jupiter is huge. It is the largest planet in the whole solar system. Want to hear another amazing fact? Jupiter has 63 moons!

Saturn

The planet Saturn has many rings. The rings are made of pieces of ice and rock. Some of the pieces are as small as marbles. Others are as big as houses!

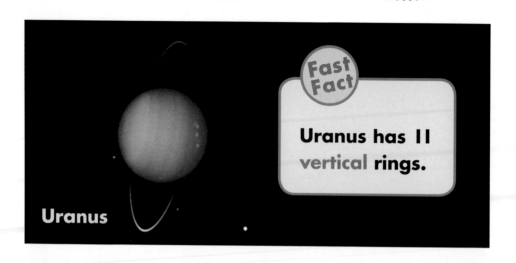

Fast Fact

Uranus has 11 vertical rings.

Uranus

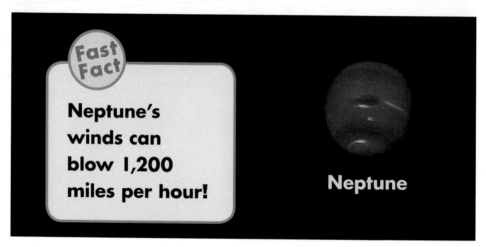

Fast Fact

Neptune's winds can blow 1,200 miles per hour!

Neptune

The planets Uranus and Neptune have a lot in common. Both are about the same size. Both are made of gas. And both are icy cold. That is because they are so far away from the sun.

Pluto

Pluto is made of a combination of rock and ice.

What is this tiny brownish ball? Pluto! Pluto is so small that scientists have decided to call it a dwarf planet instead of a regular planet. Wow! Every day we are learning brand-new things about space!

Glossary

combination (kohm-bin-**aye**-shuhn): two or more things that are put together

dwarf planet (**dworf plan**-it): a heavenly body that orbits the sun, but is smaller and different in character than a regular planet

orbit (**or**-bit): the invisible path followed by an object circling a planet or the sun

space probe (**spayss prohb**): a remote-controlled, unmanned craft that travels in space

telescope (**tel**-uh-skope): an instrument that makes faraway objects, such as planets, look closer

vertical (**vur**-tuh-kuhl): straight up and down

Comprehension Questions

1. Can you explain what a planet is in your own words?

2. Can you remember the names of all eight planets? Use this sentence to help you: *My Very Eager Mother Just Served Us Noodles.*

3. Which planet is your favorite? Tell why.